52
WEEKS

Worship Writer's Journal

52 weeks of inspirational thoughts and song starters

ISBN-13: 978-1533097262

ISBN-10: 1533097267

Sounds of the Nations
6391 Leisure Town Road
Vacaville, CA 95687
dano@missionvacaville.org

What will I get from this journal?

Songwriting Experience

Songwriters write songs. I know that sounds basic, but the truth is that many people who can write songs just don't. By following through on a specific assignment each week, you will grow stronger at songwriting and get better at what you love to do by doing what you already love to do — writing songs. I guarantee that if you write a song every week for a year and follow the songwriting tips in each lesson, *you will end up a stronger worship writer by the end of the year.*

Knowledge of Song Craft

This journal will also strengthen your understanding of song craft. In each lesson, there is a devotional thought, an assignment, a songwriting tip, and a place for you to write down your song ideas. The songwriting tips come from my thirty plus years of songwriting experience and feature material from my books, classes, and training events. In my travels around the world, I have literally empowered tens of thousands of people to write their first or best worship song. By paying attention to these tips and applying them to your songwriting, *you will be moving from self-expression to true communication through utilizing the art of song craft.*

A Deeper Relationship with God and His Word

Writing worship songs in this devotional journal format will also deepen your relationship with God. Over the course of one year, you will compose 12 prayer songs, 12 declarations of timeless truths, 12 invitations to biblical encounters and experiences in worship, and 12 songs focusing on amazing attributes of the character and nature of God. Crafting songs about the cross, baptism, salvation, healing, *abiding in Christ, the infilling of the Holy Spirit, and other **biblical topics drives you deeper into God's word and matures your relationship with Him.***

Basically, I guarantee three results if you truly follow through with this fifty-two-week devotional journal. You *will* increase your songwriting experience, you *will* improve your skill and knowledge of song craft, and you *will* deepen your relationship with God and His Word. That is a one-year commitment worth making—so let's get started.

How Do I Use This Journal?

Choose a Time and Place

Like any journal or creative exercise, it is best if you designate a specific time and place for fulfilling your assignments each week. I recommend one day a week for coming up with and capturing your initial ideas and a second day or two for refining and rewriting your song.

What if I miss a week?

Actually, I recommend that if you miss a week, you don't try to make it up. If you double-up on the assignments, you are more likely to get overwhelmed and quit your journal commitment all together. If you miss a week, simply jump back in the next week and keep writing.

Components of the Journal

Each week's assignment has six very brief sections for you to complete.

1. The Writing Assignment and Inspiration - Each week you will be assigned one of four types of worship songs: a petition song, a declaration song, an invitation song, or an adoration song. Along with the assignment, you will be given an inspirational devotional thought.

2. The Scripture Reading - Each week offers a Scripture reading. It is often from that revelation of Scripture that you will receive inspiration for the content of your song.

3. The Idea Section - After the inspirational thought and the Scripture reading, you will be asked questions and be given space to write answers that will guide you toward capturing great ideas for the construction of your song.

4. The Song Hook Section - Here you will write a phrase that sums up what your song is all about in as few words and musical notes as possible.

5. The Songwriting Tip - Each week you will receive songwriting tips that will increase your knowledge of song craft. These are the same keys that I share in song writing classes around the world.

6. The Song Idea Page - The final section for each week provides a page where you can write out lyrics to your crafted song and an additional page for those who want to write out chord charts or score their music.

A Brief Introduction to Worship Writing

Start with a Song Hook

Most great commercial songwriters identify their song hook before attempting to compose a song. The song hook tells what your song is all about in as few words and musical notes as possible. The average song hook is one to five words long. It's often the title of the song. A song hook, as its name suggests, should catch your listeners' attention, keep their interest, and take them somewhere. Composing from a song hook is the method you will use in this journal.

The Purpose of Song Sections

After you have crafted a hook, you are ready to build song sections. There are three major song sections that are the main building blocks of each song.

Verse – conveys context, content, and any vital information about your song.

Chorus – features the song hook.

Bridge – refreshes interest in the hook through musical, lyrical, and rhythmic contrast.

The Basic Song Forms in Worship

Verse/Chorus – This is the most common and popular form of our day. In this form, the verse usually comes first, and the chorus follows, emphasizing the hook through melodic or lyrical repetition. Verse/chorus song form may also use a bridge section to refresh the hook idea or a pre-chorus section to lyrically and melodically build into the hook.

AABA or Chorus/Bridge – This is the strongest song form for a song hook that doesn't require a set-up of context or information. In this song form, the song hook is the first line of the song. The second song section is called a bridge. It builds or lifts musically but does not contain the melody or lyrics of the song hook.

AAA or Chorus Only – This is the best song form for compositions with storylines or a lot of information because it features a single song section. The song hook appears as the first or last line of the song and is usually not repeated again in the song unless there are multiple versions of the one song section. AAA song form is the template most used for composing classic and modern hymns.

Tools for Building Song Sections

The three most common tools for building song sections are repetition, lists, and contrasting ideas. Let's examine each of these briefly.

Repetition – When you have a great idea or a strong line, why not just repeat it? Song craft utilizes several forms of repetition for crafting chorus sections:

- **Every Line Repetition** repeats the song hook four times.
- **Triple Repetition** repeats the song hook through three lines followed by one summation line.
- **Double or Paired Repetition** repeats the song hook twice followed by two contrasting lines.
- **Alternating Repetition** repeats the song hook every other line with contrasting lines in between.
- **First and Last Repetition** repeats the song hook in the first and last line of the song section with two complimentary lines in between.

Never be afraid to use these simple repetition tools to feature your hook in a chorus section.

Lists – These are often used for building verses, but they also appear in chorus and bridge sections of many worship songs.

- **The Key Word or Phrase List** uses a repeated phrase on each line. For example, if the key phrase was "God you are...," you might construct your verse with the following lines:

> God you are holy,
> God you are true,
> God you are faithful,
> There's none like you.

You can see that the key word or phrase list uses one repeated phrase where you essentially fill in the blank with your strongest thoughts and ideas.

- **A Unique List** features three to four original ideas in a list form:

> Faithful as the sunrise,
> Purer than the dew,
> Stronger than the mountain,
> Is God's pledge to you.

In this list form, all the ideas are connected, but no words or phrases are repeated. It is simply a unique list of complimentary ideas focused towards a single thought.

Contrasting or Opposite Ideas – These are used for any type of song section. They are probably most often used in a verse but can also form strong chorus or bridge sections. With this tool, you simply pit two contrasting or complimentary ideas against each other to build the song section:

> In my *weakness* you stood *strong*,
> When I *fell* you *carried* me,
> In my *lonely* nights a *song*,
> Jesus, you're my everything.

These three simple tools for building song sections can be identified in many of your favorite worship and marketplace songs. Don't stumble over their simplicity. These tools are the trade secrets of successful songwriters that make a song more memorable and therefore more singable.

For more complete instructions on these introductory thoughts as well as more tips and tools on songwriting, see my songwriting books and resources listed in the back of this journal.

Now, that you have acquainted or refreshed yourself with the basics of worship writing, let's begin this exciting one-year journey together!

Week 1
Write a Petition Song

Inspiration

Welcome to the first step of our one-year journey together. Let's start this year off by writing a prayer for the Spirit of wisdom and revelation so that you may know God better. Study Paul's prayer for the church of his day and watch for song hook ideas in the text.

Ephesians 1:17-19 (NIV)

17 I keep asking that the God of our Lord Jesus Christ, the glorious Father, may give you the Spirit of wisdom and revelation, so that you may know him better. **18** I pray that the eyes of your heart may be enlightened in order that you may know the hope to which he has called you, the riches of his glorious inheritance in his holy people, **19** and his incomparably great power for us who believe.

Song Idea

Before you start writing a song, really focus on what the main idea of your song is. Every great song has one great idea. The best songs have one universal song theme that everyone in your target audience can relate to. Write out one to three sentences that express the main idea of your song.

Song Hook

The song hook is the main lyrical and musical idea of the song. It should be the part of your song that gets stuck in your head and won't let you go. The song hook contains the main idea of the song in as few words and musical notes as possible presented in one well-stated word or phrase. Write your song hook idea in one to five words in the space below.

Songwriting Tip

In a sung petition, the song hook should be in the form of a request or prayer.

Title:

Music and Lyrics by:

Title:

Music and Lyrics by:

Week 2

Write a Declaration Song

Inspiration

Singing biblical truth is an essential part of fulfilling our call to serve as worship writers and as true worshippers. Declaration songs are meant to do more for us than just state what we believe; they give us the opportunity for a continuing experience with a spiritual revelation. In the passage below, Paul's writings celebrate the cross as one of the greatest truths in human history. Meditate on what the cross means to you and how you might express this truth in a declaration song.

Galatians 6:14 (NIV)

14 May I never boast except in the cross of our Lord Jesus Christ, through which the world has been crucified to me, and I to the world.

Song Idea

Familiarity with a topic can sometimes make it difficult to write something fresh. Take those opportunities to dig deep and find new language and genuine passion for a timeless truth. Write a few sentences below about what the cross really means to you personally.

Song Hook

Craft your ideas into one central theme or clearly-stated statement of one to five words. Write that song hook below.

Songwriting Tip

One of the universal creative writing rules is, "Show us; don't tell us." Make sure your lyrics are creating emotions and encounters not just stating truth.

Title:

Music and Lyrics by:

Title:

Music and Lyrics by:

Week 3
Write an Invitation Song

Inspiration

Invitation songs encourage us to praise or worship God with a specific biblical expression. The Bible is filled with these biblical invitations, inspiring us to worship the Lord in very specific ways and for a variety of reasons. Read through and meditate on the biblical invitation below.

Psalm 95:1-5 (NIV)

Come, let us sing for joy to the Lord;

   let us shout aloud to the Rock of our salvation.

2 Let us come before him with thanksgiving

   and extol him with music and song.

3 For the Lord is the great God,

   the great King above all gods.

4 In his hand are the depths of the earth,

and the mountain peaks belong to him.

5 The sea is his, for he made it,

and his hands formed the dry land.

Song Idea

Let's focus on the invitation to shout to the Rock of our salvation. What are the revelations of God that would inspire this specific response in your life? Write your thoughts below.

Song Hook

Craft a song hook that contains an invitation to shout.

Songwriting Tip

An invitation song is crafted in two main sections. One section contains the invitation; the second section gives the reasons that inspire that action. Although you definitely could compose this song using the standard Verse/Chorus song form (and you are totally free to do so), I recommend experimenting with the AABA or Chorus/Bridge song form for this assignment.

Title:

Music and Lyrics by:

Title:

Music and Lyrics by:

Week 4
Write an Adoration Song

Inspiration

Congratulations on reaching the final week of your first month in this worship writer's journal. This week, your focus will be songs of adoration. Adoration songs use first person pronouns that bring us face-to-face in worship of God and usually focus specifically on one attribute or quality of the character and nature of God. God being revealed as our Heavenly Father is one of the greatest and most transformational revelations of God in Scripture.

Galatians 4:6-7 (NIV)

6 Because you are his sons, God sent the Spirit of his Son into our hearts, the Spirit who calls out, " *Abba*, Father."
7 So you are no longer a slave, but God's child; and since you are his child, God has made you also an heir.

Song Idea

How would you highlight the father characteristics of God in a song? What are some of God's most father-like qualities that you personally relate to?

Song Hook

Your hook should express adoration of God as Father.

Songwriting Tip

You can build great verse sections by using the simple list method. For this assignment, you could list three or four father-like qualities in each verse and compose your chorus using repetition of the song hook adoring God as Father.

Title:

Music and Lyrics by:

Title:

Music and Lyrics by:

Week 5
Write a Petition Song

Inspiration

This week, our prayer focus will be on power. Though many in our world today crave power, power in itself isn't evil. The question is what kind of power do you seek? Apostle Paul prayed that the Church might experience the power of the Spirit and then listed some of the reasons why. Meditate on what this power is and what this power can do for you.

Ephesians 3:16-19 (NIV)

16 I pray that out of his glorious riches he may strengthen you with power through his Spirit in your inner being, 17 so that Christ may dwell in your hearts through faith. And I pray that you, being rooted and established in love, 18 may have

power, together with all the Lord's holy people, to grasp how wide and long and high and deep is the love of Christ, **19** and to know this love that surpasses knowledge—that you may be filled to the measure of all the fullness of God.

Song Idea

What kind of power should we be praying for, and what can it do for us? Write below the answers inspired from Scripture along with your own ideas and inspirations.

Song Hook

Remember that the song hook of a petition song is in the form of a request. Write the summation of your ideas above in one catchy cry for power.

Songwriting Tip

Many famous songwriters compose their melody a cappella, that is without the accompaniment of a musical instrument. This keeps your melody idea from being bound to a specific chord structure.

Title:

Music and Lyrics by:

_____

_____

_____

_____

_____

_____

_____

_____

_____

_____

_____

_____

_____

_____

_____

_____

_____

Title:

Music and Lyrics by:

Week 6
Write a Declaration Song

Inspiration

Have you ever thought of baptism as your own burial service? Burial gives us closure with the one who has passed. In our world of medical advances when someone dies, there is a chance that he or she could be revived from death. However, once one is buried, there is no possible resuscitation apart from resurrection by the power of Jesus Christ. Through baptism, we make closure with our old self, habits, and sin, and then are raised up a new creation. Meditate on the following Scripture and declare your identification with Christ through baptism and the finality of your new creation.

Romans 6:1-4 (NIV)

1 What shall we say, then? Shall we go on sinning so that grace may increase? 2 By no means! We are those who

have died to sin; how can we live in it any longer? **3** Or don' t you know that all of us who were baptized into Christ Jesus were baptized into his death? **4** We were therefore buried with him through baptism into death in order that, just as Christ was raised from the dead through the glory of the Father, we too may live a new life.

Song Idea

Death is a morbid subject and not one that we often sing about. The challenge here is to express the power of baptism through song in a way that is not typical, morbid, or depressing. What do you want to declare about the power of a true baptism experience? Write your ideas below.

Song Hook

Craft a song hook that relates directly to the subject of baptism.

Songwriting Tip

Metaphors are a powerful way to express truth. Rather than sing the word baptism, what word pictures might you use to say the same thing in a more picturesque and singable form?

Title:

Music and Lyrics by:

Title:

Music and Lyrics by:

Week 7
Write an Invitation Song

Inspiration

The very first act of worship in the Bible involved bowing and kneeling. To bow also relates to the most literal interpretation of worship in the New Testament. When was the last time you just humbled yourself in the presence of the Lord and worshipped by kneeling or bowing?

Psalm 95:6-7 (NIV)

6 Come, let us bow down in worship,

 let us kneel before the Lord our Maker;

7 for he is our God

 and we are the people of his pasture,

 the flock under his care.

Song Idea

Remember that an invitation song has two song sections. The hook section contains the invitation; the second section expresses the reasons or revelations that inspire that specific response. What revelations of God make you want to bow and worship Him? Write your ideas below.

Song Hook

Now craft a song hook that is an invitation to bow, kneel, or get low before Almighty God.

Songwriting Tip

Word pictures and images inspire passionate responses. Picture your lyrics as the script for a music video. This will help with the "show me; don't tell me" rule of great songwriting.

Title:

Music and Lyrics by:

Title:

Music and Lyrics by:

Week 8
Write an Adoration Song

Inspiration

One of the greatest recorded corporate worship services in all of the Bible occurred at the dedication of Solomon's temple. Can you imagine what it was like for God's glory to fill the temple in such a way that everyone there was utterly and totally overwhelmed by the presence of God?

2 Chronicles 5:13-14 (NIV)

13 The trumpeters and musicians joined in unison to give praise and thanks to the Lord. Accompanied by trumpets, cymbals and other instruments, the singers raised their voices in praise to the Lord and sang: " He is good; his love endures forever." Then the temple of the Lord was filled with the cloud, 14 and the priests could not perform their

service because of the cloud, for the glory of the Lord filled the temple of God.

Song Idea

As they sang of God's goodness, the glory of God manifested. The goodness of God is honored hundreds of times in Scripture, and the revelation of God's goodness has accompanied more than one supernatural encounter. When you think of the goodness of God, what thoughts come to mind? How has God's goodness manifested or been revealed to you? Write your answers below.

Song Hook

Remember that adoration songs use first person pronoun's, e.g. "You are..." Compose a song hook that adores God for His goodness in a fresh or unique way.

Songwriting Tip

Successful songs feature the song hook, and repetition is the most common and fundamental way in which to do this. Don't be afraid to use repetition because it is simple.

Title:

Music and Lyrics by:

Title:

Music and Lyrics by:

Week 9
Write a Petition Song

Inspiration

Love is that quality that most completely and succinctly describes God for God is love. Experientially knowing, encountering, and expressing God's love are the keys to living an abundant life. That's why Paul the Apostle prayed for the Church of his day to know this love more and more.

Philippians 1:9-10 (NIV)

9 And this is my prayer: that your love may abound more and more in knowledge and depth of insight, 10 so that you may be able to discern what is best and may be pure and blameless for the day of Christ,

Song Idea

What do you most long for concerning the love of God? Do you want to feel it more, understand it more, see it more, or express it to others better? Write your greatest desires concerning the love of God in the space below.

Song Hook

Craft your best ideas above into one petition concerning the love of God that will form your song hook.

Songwriting Tip

Rhyme abuse takes on many forms. The most obvious example is when we compose a line of a song purely for the purpose of rhyming it with another line. Always write what you truly want to say first. Make sure your content is strong and sincere. Then rewrite your lines to form combinations of perfect and imperfect rhymes that beautifully frame the true essence of what you want to say.

Title:

Music and Lyrics by:

Title:

Music and Lyrics by:

Week 10
Write a Declaration Song

Inspiration

The original writer composed Psalm 96 as an invitation song. In it, however, he embedded the command to proclaim God's salvation every day. As we have learned, a declaration song can be a proclamation of essential truths. A declaration song can also contain a proclamation of intent. Picture yourself on a stage with a massive, live crowd and an even larger televised audience. You have one song to declare the glory and goodness of your salvation experience to a global audience. What would you sing?

Psalm 96:1-3 (NIV)

1 Sing to the Lord a new song; sing to the Lord, all the earth.

2 Sing to the Lord, praise his name; proclaim his salvation day after day.

3 Declare his glory among the nations, his marvelous deeds among all peoples.

Song Idea

The Greek word for salvation is "sozo." It refers to salvation, healing, deliverance, prosperity, and the full abundant life that Christ purchased for us. What descriptors would you use to testify and declare the joy of your salvation? Write your thoughts below.

Song Hook

A declaration song hook can be a statement of intent like, "I will ..." Craft below a song hook that is a declaration of your intention to proclaim or celebrate your salvation.

Songwriting Tip

Remember that a song hook expresses what your song is all about in as few words and music notes as possible. The average song hook is one to five potent words.

Title:

Music and Lyrics by:

Title:

Music and Lyrics by:

Week 11
Write an Invitation Song

Inspiration

Hype happens when we ask people to perform a certain act of praise without first inspiring that response. Whenever we sing or attempt to praise God without real revelation of what we are doing or singing, we risk increasing the spirit of religion. As a worship leader or songwriter, commanding the people to dance before the Lord doesn't usually turn out well. Consider what revelations would inspire people to dance before God.

Psalm 149:2-4 (NIV)

Let Israel rejoice in their Maker;

  let the people of Zion be glad in their King.

3 Let them praise his name with dancing

  and make music to him with timbrel and harp.

Song Idea

There are many forms or styles of dancing. Each type of dance is inspired by a different type of music. Picture what form of dancing you see people doing before God and craft lyrics and music that would inspire that response. Capture your ideas in the space below.

Song Hook

Write a song hook below that is a compelling invitation to dance before or with God.

Songwriting Tip

Prosody is the marriage between melody and prose. In simple terms, it means that your song should sound like what it says. When a song possesses great prosody, you can hear the music without the lyrics and still capture the essence of what it is saying. In this exercise, your music must be danceable.

Title:

Music and Lyrics by:

Title:

Music and Lyrics by:

Week 12
Write an Adoration Song

Inspiration

Romans 1 reveals that what can be known about God can be clearly seen through what He has created. That's an amazing insight. Creation declares everything knowable about God. Perhaps this is why the verses below teach us that God is to forever be praised as Creator.

Romans 1:19-20, 25 (NIV)

19 since what may be known about God is plain to them, because God has made it plain to them. **20** For since the creation of the world God's invisible qualities—his eternal power and divine nature—have been clearly seen, being understood from what has been made, so that people are without excuse... **25** They exchanged the truth about God for a lie, and worshiped and served created things rather than the Creator—who is forever praised. Amen.

Song Idea

What aspects of creation inspire worship in you? What have you learned about God through what He has created? Capture your best ideas in the space below.

Song Hook

Craft a first person adoration song hook of God as Creator in the space below.

Songwriting Tip

I recommend using a unique list of your best images from creation for the verses and using the response of adoration for your chorus. Let your strongest ideas determine the best song structure to use.

Title:

Music and Lyrics by:

Title:

Music and Lyrics by:

Week 13
Freestyle Writing

Inspiration

Congratulations on completing the first three months of purposeful worship writing. As you work on each assignment, you are broadening your understanding of the primary types of worship songs. Your are growing in the skill of translating spiritual truths into singable lyrics and melodies. Your knowledge of song craft expands with each completed lesson. Imagine your growth at the end of the year! Keep pressing through with your commitment to write a song every week for one year.

As a reward for your hard work, this week you get a freestyle writing assignment. You can write whatever song form and type you want to. Today's Scripture reference is an encouragement for you. I believe just opening ourselves up for inspiration from heaven each week invites God to fill us with His goodness.

Psalm 81:10 (NIV)

I am the Lord your God, who brought you up out of Egypt.
Open wide your mouth and I will fill it.

Song Idea

Start with a clear understanding of what you want to
communicate. Who is your audience? What is your central
idea?

Song Hook

Great songs start with great song hooks. Expressing your
song idea in as few words and musical notes as possible,
write your central idea below.

Songwriting Tip

John Wimber of Vineyard Music said, "Great songs are not
written, they are rewritten, rewritten, rewritten." Never be
afraid to improve on your initial great idea through
rewriting.

Title:

Music and Lyrics by:

Title:

Music and Lyrics by:

Week 14
Write a Petition Song

Inspiration

Every good father dreams of what his children might be or do. He desires the best things in life for his kids. God the Father dreams about you. He desires great things to come your way. The knowledge of God's will is not necessarily something for you to do but rather an understanding of God's thoughts, intentions, and good pleasure towards you.

Colossians 1:9-12 (NIV)

9 For this reason, since the day we heard about you, we have not stopped praying for you. We continually ask God to fill you with the knowledge of his will through all the wisdom and understanding that the Spirit gives, 10 so that you may live a life worthy of the Lord and please him in every way:

bearing fruit in every good work, growing in the knowledge of God, **11** being strengthened with all power according to his glorious might so that you may have great endurance and patience, **12** and giving joyful thanks to the Father, who has qualified you to share in the inheritance of his holy people in the kingdom of light.

Song Idea

The quest to know God's will does not need to become years of agonizing searching. God's Word spells out many things that reveal His will for every person. What things do you know God desires for every person to know and experience? Write your ideas below.

Song Hook

A petition song hook captures a specific measurable request usually in the form of a question. What are you asking God concerning the knowledge of His will? Craft your song hook below.

Songwriting Tip

A series of contrasting or opposite ideas can be used to create a strong verse section.

Title:

Music and Lyrics by:

_____

_____

_____

_____

_____

_____

_____

_____

_____

_____

_____

_____

_____

_____

_____

_____

_____

_____

_____

_____

_____

Copyright is Today's Date:

Title:

Music and Lyrics by:

Week 15
Write a Declaration Song

Inspiration

In 2011, Bryan and Katie Torwalt crafted the declaration "Holy Spirit you are welcome here" that earned a 2015 Dove award nomination for Worship Song of the Year. I think the popularity of this song shows the hunger of people to know the power of the Holy Spirit. God's desire for every believer is to totally fill them with the same Spirit that fills God Himself (Ephesians 3:19).

Acts 1:8 (NIV)

But you will receive power when the Holy Spirit comes on you; and you will be my witnesses in Jerusalem, and in all Judea and Samaria, and to the ends of the earth."

Song Idea

Craft a declaration song about the Holy Spirit. Choose whether you will make this song a declaration of truth or a declaration of intent. A declaration of truth might explore all the benefits of being filled with the Spirit, e.g. "He will..." A declaration of intent might be your response to His infilling, e.g. "I will.." Choose your declaration target and capture your ideas below.

Song Hook

Because Holy Spirit is our subject target, make sure that your song hook directly references Him.

Songwriting Tip

A song is not a sermon with three to five points. A song has one central theme clearly stated in a song hook. All other ideas in the song must point directly towards your song hook. Don't let your song become a tangle of competing ideas. Focus every thought at the target of your one best idea.

Title:

Music and Lyrics by:

Title:

Music and Lyrics by:

Week 16
Write an Invitation Song

Inspiration

Ephesians chapter six features the armor of God. Many people stop at verse seventeen and never realize that prayer serves as one of the most essential and uniting forces of this armor. I call the theme of verses 18-19 "the allness of prayer." Look at how many times a form of the word "all" appears in these two short verses.

Ephesians 6:18-19a (NIV)

18 And pray in the Spirit on all occasions with all kinds of prayers and requests. With this in mind, be alert and always keep on praying for all the Lord's people. 19 Pray also for me,

Song Idea

With these things in mind, your assignment this week is to issue a call to prayer. While we know that one song section will contain the invitation to pray, the second section might contain the benefits of prayer, the reasons for prayer, or several prayer needs that would inspire prayer. Express your song focus in a few sentences below.

Song Hook

What is the hook within your call to prayer? Write it in the space below.

Songwriting Tip

Though this journal's assignments focus on spiritual themes, try to write songs that are free of religious jargon or terminology that only seasoned Christians would understand. Don't let your language narrow your audience.

Title:

Music and Lyrics by:

Title:

Music and Lyrics by:

Week 17
Write an Adoration Song

Inspiration

I read once that there are over 120 descriptions of God in Scripture. Each description should be taken as an opportunity for adoration. When we worship God, we invite an encounter based upon the specific quality or attribute we are focusing on. In John chapters four and seven, God reveals Himself as the Living Water. Have you ever been desperately thirsty? Have you experienced the same level of thirst in your spiritual life?

John 7:37-38 (NIV)

37 On the last and greatest day of the festival, Jesus stood and said in a loud voice, "Let anyone who is thirsty come to me and drink. 38 Whoever believes in me, as Scripture has said, rivers of living water will flow from within them."

Song Idea

This might be a good place to capture ideas that formulate feelings of thirst in the listener. What word pictures make you physically or spiritually thirsty? Capture your best ideas below.

Song Hook

Your song hook below should feature a first person adoration of God as the Living Water. Write as though you are speaking directly to Him.

Songwriting Tip

Great songs will often utilize two or more song craft techniques. Try using repetition for the chorus of this song. For the verse, try a list of your best word pictures inspiring a spiritual thirst or use multiple contrasting ideas that take us from thirst to satisfaction.

Title:

Music and Lyrics by:

77

Title:

Music and Lyrics by:

Week 18
Write a Petition Song

Inspiration

Hope is one of the greatest commodities of a joy-filled life. Martin Luther, the great reformer of the sixteenth century said, "Everything that is done in the world is done by hope." How does the Apostle Paul tell us that we can overflow with this world-changing hope?

Romans 15:13 (NIV)

13 May the God of hope fill you with all joy and peace as you trust in him, so that you may overflow with hope by the power of the Holy Spirit.

Song Idea

What are some things you are hoping for? Now think on a bigger scale. What are things that every person hopes for? How are these things found in God? Write your ideas below.

Song Hook

The focus of your song assignment is hope, but your song hook may contain Paul's petition, "Fill us with joy and peace... so that..." Craft your petition song hook below.

Songwriting Tip

Memorable melodies are a key to great songs. To test the catchiness of your melody, play your song hook or chorus for a person one time. After one hearing, do they whistle, hum, or sing the melody? If so, you've got a memorable song hook that will stay with people for a long time.

Title:

Music and Lyrics by:

Title:

Music and Lyrics by:

Week 19
Write a Declaration Song

Inspiration

Songs about friends have dominated the billboard charts throughout the years — everything from The Beatles' "With a Little Help From My Friends," to Randy Newman's "You Got a Friend in Me," to The White Stripes' "We're Going to Be Friends." It's clear that people are hungry for friendship. How astounding is it that we have been offered the best friendship in the universe through our relationship with God in Christ?

John 15:15 (NIV)

15 I no longer call you servants, because a servant does not know his master's business. Instead, I have called you friends, for everything that I learned from my Father I have made known to you.

Song Idea

The phrase "friends with benefits" was not coined as a godly term, but this is a great chance to meditate on the benefits of friendship with God. Record some of those benefits below.

Song Hook

By now, you should be familiar with two of the different forms of declaration songs: declaration of truth and declaration of intent. This week we will add a declaration of identity. Song hooks that declare identity often start with words like "I am..." or "We are..." When referring to God, a declaration song will use the third person "He is..." in contrast to the adoration song which uses the first person "You are..." Practice crafting a song hook that uses a declaration of identity.

Songwriting Tip

Every word in your song should be important. One way to make sure your lyric is strong is to look closely at your song and cross out every word that is not absolutely necessary. Now go back through the song and rebuild your flow, replacing weak words with stronger verbs and descriptors.

Title:

Music and Lyrics by:

Title:

Music and Lyrics by:

Week 20
Write an Invitation Song

Inspiration

Great songwriters know their target audience. I know a famous worship writer who tries to picture the congregation singing his chorus. If he can hear them singing it, then he knows it will communicate to their hearts successfully. For this assignment our invitation will be to the lost. We want to make an appeal to know and be reconciled with God.

2 Corinthians 5:19-21 (NIV)

19 that God was reconciling the world to himself in Christ, not counting people's sins against them. And he has committed to us the message of reconciliation. **20** We are therefore Christ's ambassadors, as though God were making his appeal through us. We implore you on Christ's behalf: Be reconciled to God. **21** God made him who had no sin to be sin for us, so that in him we might become the righteousness of God.

Song Idea

A great challenge for those of us who have been followers of Jesus for a while is to resist the urge to preach or teach in a song. How can you invite people to know Christ without using any religious language at all? In the space below, write down some foundational reasons to know Christ and then develop unique and relatable ways to say the same thing in a song line that anyone could understand.

Song Hook

Craft your invitation for the lost to know Christ in the form of a song hook.

Songwriting Tip

Rhyme abuse number two: rhyming too many lines. Unless you are composing a rap song, you probably want to alternate rhyming lines with non-rhyming ones.

Title:

Music and Lyrics by:

Title:

Music and Lyrics by:

Week 21
Write an Adoration Song

Inspiration

When you hear the words, "God is a consuming fire," what do you think of? Out of context, this phrase could really scare you. However, the Book of Hebrews makes it clear that we are not coming to an untouchable place of fear, darkness, and gloom. Through Christ, we come to a living God, a heavenly city, and a joyful assembly. In that context, we recognize God as a consuming fire with reverence and awe.

Hebrews 12:18, 22, 28-29 (NIV)

18 You have not come to a mountain that can be touched and that is burning with fire; to darkness, gloom and storm... 22 But you have come to Mount Zion, to the city of the living God, the heavenly Jerusalem. You have come to thousands upon thousands of angels in joyful assembly...28 Therefore,

since we are receiving a kingdom that cannot be shaken, let us be thankful, and so worship God acceptably with reverence and awe, **29** for our "God is a consuming fire."

Song Idea

In what positive ways is God a consuming fire? Write your ideas below.

Song Hook

Craft your song hook to adore God as a consuming fire in the space provided below.

Songwriting Tip

Adoration songs are meant to bring us near to God or to encounter God. Make sure that your language and imagery do not create distance while inspiring awe and reverence. With the exception of break-up songs, great songwriters most often attempt to put their subjects in a positive light.

Title:

Music and Lyrics by:

Title:

Music and Lyrics by:

Week 22
Write a Petition Song

Inspiration

Unity is a powerful concept. In the New Testament, the two primary words for unity, agreement and one accord, both imply a musical reference. "Agree" is the Greek word *"symphōneō."* Much like our English word symphony, it means "to be harmonious." "One accord" is the Greek word *"homothymadon."* The Greek lexicon defines it this way:

> The image is almost musical; a number of notes are sounded which, while different, harmonize in pitch and tone. As the instruments of a great concert under the direction of a concert master, so the Holy Spirit blends together the lives of members of Christ's church.

Understanding these things, it seems appropriate that musicians would call for agreement, unity, and coming together in one accord in the Church.

Romans 15:5-6 (NIV)

5 May the God who gives endurance and encouragement give you the same attitude of mind toward each other that Christ Jesus had, **6** so that with one mind and one voice you may glorify the God and Father of our Lord Jesus Christ.

Song Idea

One way to compose songs inspired by Scripture is to research them in other translations or paraphrases. I enjoy the non-religious language of The Message Bible and The New Living Translation. Use an online tool like Biblegateway.com to see this passage in other versions. Write down the phrases that might make good lines in a song in the space below.

Song Hook

Craft a song hook in the space below that is a prayer for unity.

Songwriting Tip

Great song lyrics have balanced symmetry. Symmetry speaks of a pleasing proportion of parts, a similar or exact correspondence between different things. One way to achieve symmetry in your song lyrics is to match the syllable counts between alternating lines.

Title:

Music and Lyrics by:

Title:

Music and Lyrics by:

Week 23
Write a Declaration Song

Inspiration

Some people claim that Christians should never be spiritually hungry. While I agree that we need to be thankful for what we have and that the fullness of God is already fully in us, there still is that cry in our hearts to be more aware of all that we have in Him, to walk more completely in its fullness, and to more deeply grasp the greatness of what we have in God. Paul the Apostle shared this paradox of taking hold of that which has already been taken hold of for us in Christ.

Philippians 3:12 (NIV)

Not that I have already obtained all this, or have already arrived at my goal, but I press on to take hold of that for which Christ Jesus took hold of me.

Song Idea

What things are you trying to take hold of that Christ has already taken hold of for you? What are the obstacles you face in breaking through these areas? How might you sing these things? Try to craft a declaration song that shows this hunger but does not depict hopelessness or distance from God. Write your ideas below.

Song Hook

A declaration of intent might be a good choice for this song. Consider adapting Philippians 3:12-13 or a paraphrase thereof to craft your song hook below.

Songwriting Tip

Contrast is a key to great songwriting both lyrically and melodically. In the melody, contrast is most often seen at the end of verse lines. If your first line goes up in melody you may want the second line to go down. The third line would then go up and the fourth line would build into your chorus.

Title:

Music and Lyrics by:

Title:

Music and Lyrics by:

Week 24
Write an Invitation Song

Inspiration

Invitation songs are not limited to people. We can invite angels or even creation to join in the praise of our God. This thought is expressed in the following psalm.

1 Chronicles 16:31 (NIV)

Let the heavens rejoice, let the earth be glad; let them say among the nations, "The Lord reigns!"

Song Idea

Your assignment this week is to create an invitation song to heaven or earth (not people.) This exercise is part of broadening your perspective and expanding your writing skill. In the space below, write out who or what your target is and what action you are calling for.

Song Hook

Craft your song hook as an invitation to your target audience in the space below.

Songwriting Tip

Those who perform worship songs often use charts rather than scored music. In sheet music, you can mark where there is a rest or indicate the dynamics of a song. These are harder to indicate on a chord chart, but dynamics still should be a part of your consideration in songwriting. A well placed rest can really set up the emphasis of a song hook or memorable moment within your song. Watch for places you might insert a dramatic pause or rest.

Title:

Music and Lyrics by:

Title:

Music and Lyrics by:

Week 25
Write an Adoration Song

Inspiration

One of the most common descriptions of God in heavenly realms is the Lord God Almighty. It is used nine times in the Book of Revelation. In the Greek language, "almighty" is the powerful sounding word "*pantokratōr*." It literally means "he who holds sway over all things, the ruler of all, holding all power, strength, and dominion." Taking heavenly songs, revelations, and images and translating them into our earthly worship experience can be a very powerful exercise. Take a moment to imagine yourself in the heavenly worship service described in Revelation 4:8.

Revelation 4:8 (NIV)

Each of the four living creatures had six wings and was covered with eyes all around, even under its wings. Day and night they never stop saying: 'Holy, holy, holy is the Lord God Almighty,' who was, and is, and is to come."

Song Idea

Take this concept of the Lord God Almighty and put it to song. What images come to mind when you meditate on the meaning of Almighty? Write your ideas below.

Song Hook

Craft this heavenly title into an earthly song hook for adoration in the space provided.

Songwriting Tip

Who are you talking too? Novice songwriters often switch personal perspective and pronouns in the middle of their songs. For example, the verses might be third person, "He is.." and the chorus first/second person, "I will... for You are..." That gets confusing. Speak to your audience in a consistent tense.

Title:

Music and Lyrics by:

Title:

Music and Lyrics by:

Week 26
Freestyle Writing

Inspiration

Congratulations on reaching another milestone in your commitment to a year of worship writing. Wow! Six months have flown by. You have crafted six prayer songs to God, encouraged six powerful expressions of worship, and made six life-changing declarations. As well, you have wisely spent time adoring six attributes of God. This isn't just about song writing—you are deepening your worship experience. Over this six months, you have been training to be one who worships in Spirit and in truth. Keep pressing on and visualizing the strength of your writing and relationship with God at the end of this one-year journey. Way to go!

John 4:23-24 (NIV)

23 Yet a time is coming and has now come when the true worshipers will worship the Father in the Spirit and in truth, for they are the kind of worshipers the Father seeks. **24** God is spirit, and his worshipers must worship in the Spirit and in truth."

Song Idea

Today, capture the freshest revelation on your heart. What most excites you about your journey with God in this season? Choose the most appropriate of the four worship song types to capture your song idea below.

Song Hook

By now, you're getting great at crafting strong song hooks. Write below a song hook that is appropriate for the song type you have chosen this week.

Songwriting Tip

What do you do when a song could fit in more than one of our four types of worship songs? The answer is the song hook determines what type of song it is. If the verse lyrics are a declaration while the song hook is a request, then the song is a petition song. The hook always determines the song type.

Title:

Music and Lyrics by:

Title:

Music and Lyrics by:

Week 27
Write a Petition Song

Inspiration

Proverbs 4:23 advises us, "Above all else, guard your heart, for everything you do flows from it." During the years I toured as a young musician, I think the greatest challenge was keeping my heart right and not letting it grow critical, cynical, or careless. The enemy of our souls keeps a constant barrage of hurts, offenses, distractions, and fears coming our way. We can't merely take a defensive position, but must allow Holy Spirit to keep strengthening and positioning our hearts in endless encounters with the love of God. Increasing and overflowing in love is the key to a strong and healthy heart.

1 Thessalonians 3:12-13 (NIV)

12 May the Lord make your love increase and overflow for each other and for everyone else, just as ours does for you.

13 May he strengthen your hearts so that you will be blameless and holy in the presence of our God and Father when our Lord Jesus comes with all his holy ones.

Song Idea

When I craft a song inspired by Scripture, I look for powerful words that might form the seeds of a great song hook. Read through the verse above a few times and circle the words that jump out at you.

Song Hook

Choose the circled word that sparks the best song idea in you and craft a petition song hook from it in the space below.

Songwriting Tip

Song hooks can benefit from an outside source like a thesaurus. If the petition hook you chose was, "Strengthen my heart," then search the thesaurus to see if there are any synonyms that express the idea in a more singable form. In this case you would find words like: enlarge, establish, increase, restore, sustain, empower, fortify, temper, tone, and fuel the fire. Even if you don't find a verb that you like better, this practice tends to broaden your depth of understanding of the idea which in turn can help you craft a better song.

Title:

Music and Lyrics by:

Copyright is Today's Date:

117

Title:

Music and Lyrics by:

Week 28
Write a Declaration Song

One of the great disciplines of a busy life is learning how to stay present in the moment. When we come home from work to our family or friends, we shouldn't bring all the thoughts and concerns of work with us. Learning to be fully present in the moment is a key to understanding Jesus' various repetitions of the instruction to "remain in..."

John 15:7-10 (NIV)

7 If you remain in me and my words remain in you, ask whatever you wish, and it will be done for you. 8 This is to my Father's glory, that you bear much fruit, showing yourselves to be my disciples. 9 As the Father has loved me, so have I loved you. Now remain in my love. 10 If you keep my commands, you will remain in my love, just as I have kept my Father's commands and remain in his love.

Song Idea

When a phrase is repeated in Scripture, it emphasizes the main point of the passage. We have already identified that the phrase "remain in..." is repeated several times. In the space below make a list of the "remain in" phrases. Meditate on how these phrases might be crafted into a song idea.

Song Hook

In his worship classic, *Exploring Worship*, author Bob Sorge says that our experience will always rise to the level of our declaration. This is the power of a declaration song. It's a great idea to turn God's commands or instructions into declarations of intent. Take a command phrase from the list above and craft it into your commitment to respond with a hook that begins with "I will..."

Songwriting Tip

Great songs motivate us to sing their message. If your song doesn't inspire you, then it's not finished. Keep working on it.

Title:

Music and Lyrics by:

Title:

Music and Lyrics by:

Week 29
Write an Invitation Song

Inspiration

Whenever I get edgy, weary, or anxious, I'm reminded to check my awareness of and sensitivity to God's presence. Like a television antenna or a microphone cable, the clarity of the picture or sound depends upon the quality of my connection. How is your connection with God today?

Matthew 11:28-29 (NIV)

28 "Come to me, all you who are weary and burdened, and I will give you rest. 29 Take my yoke upon you and learn from me, for I am gentle and humble in heart, and you will find rest for your souls."

Song Idea

Develop some song ideas by contrasting the difference between rest and anxiety. Make one list that says "when I'm rested I feel..., " and another that says "without rest I feel....

Song Hook

Craft a song hook inviting people to experience rest for their souls.

Songwriting Tip

Strong songwriters should avoid being intentionally or unintentionally obscure in their songs. Get to the point of the lyric within the first two lines or sentences. If you don't know what your song is all about then neither will others. Every line of your song should contribute to the main idea.

Title:

Music and Lyrics by:

Title:

Music and Lyrics by:

Week 30
Write an Adoration Song

Inspiration

The title, Lord, appears over 7,000 times in Scripture. As such, it is one of the most frequently mentioned names of God. Have you ever really taken the time to meditate upon what this title means in a modern context? Whenever we sing a worship song without a true revelation of the lyric, we risk callusing our hearts. Meditate on what the word Lord really means to you.

Romans 10:9 (NIV)

If you declare with your mouth, "Jesus is Lord,"   and believe in your heart that God raised him from the dead, you will be saved.

Song Idea

Capture your meditations on Christ as Lord in the space below. What ideas did you come up with for the question, "What does His lordship mean to you?"

Song Hook

Your assignment this week is to craft an adoration song focused on the lordship of Jesus Christ. Remember that an adoration song uses personal pronouns. Craft your hook idea below.

Songwriting Tip

The average worship song has only eight to twelve unique lines. Longer is not stronger. Write enough to completely express your idea, but don't be afraid to repeat powerful lines more than once.

Title:

Music and Lyrics by:

Title:

Music and Lyrics by:

Week 31
Write an Invitation Song

Inspiration

One of the things I find fascinating in Scripture is how God loves dreamers—the Josephs, the Davids, and the Daniels. There are always those who focus only on their current reality. Others live and dream in a world of fantasy. God's champions are the courageous few who by His power, grace, and favor, turn their dreams into reality.

2 Thessalonians 1:11-12 (NIV)

11 With this in mind, we constantly pray for you, that our God may make you worthy of his calling, and that by his power he may bring to fruition your every desire for goodness and your every deed prompted by faith. 12 We pray this so that the name of our Lord Jesus may be glorified

in you, and you in him, according to the grace of our God and the Lord Jesus Christ.

Song Idea

God wants to empower you to bring to fruition every good desire and every deed prompted by faith. List below some of the desires and deeds you dream of fulfilling in Him. Consider how you might lift these things to the Lord in song.

Song Hook

Formulate a petition song hook below that is based on the promise of the above Scripture and the deeds and desires you dream of.

Songwriting Tip

Your song can upgrade from being personal to you to being applicable to anyone, anywhere — we call that a universal song theme. The challenge for the writer is to stay truly personally invested in the lyric and melody while seeking expression that has universal appeal.

Title:

Music and Lyrics by:

Title:

Music and Lyrics by:

Week 32
Write a Declaration Song

Inspiration

Psalm 119 is the longest praise and worship song in the Bible. This psalm is an acrostic poem where each stanza begins with successive letters of the Hebrew alphabet. In this song, I'm often impressed by how the writer declares his undying passion for God's word, His law, and His commands. We live under an even better covenant than those of the Old Testament. Our New Testament covenant is full of love, grace, and blessings. When was the last time you expressed your love and devotion for God's word?

Psalm 119:19-20 (NIV)

18 Open my eyes that I may see wonderful things in your law. 19 I am a stranger on earth; do not hide your

commands from me. **20** My soul is consumed with longing for your laws at all times.

Song Idea

Compose a few lines of your own that articulate your love and devotion to God's Word.

Song Hook

What a radical declaration the psalmist made when saying, "My soul is consumed with longing for your laws at all times." What declaration do you want to make to God concerning your relationship to His Word? Form that commitment into your song hook in the space below.

Songwriting Tip

Sometimes we are tempted to pen lyrics with multiple syllables or tongue-twisting alliteration. Remember that a great song doesn't just read well, it must be singable.

Title:

Music and Lyrics by:

Title:

Music and Lyrics by:

Week 33
Write an Invitation Song

Inspiration

One of the greatest invitation songs in worship history appears at Christmas time each year. Originally composed in 1743 by John Wade, it was translated from Latin to English in 1841 by Frederick Oakeley. The chorus offers the timeless invitation, "O come, let us adore Him." Though the word "adore" never appears in Scripture, it sums up the essence of extravagant worship and speaks to a deep place in the hearts of believers across the centuries. When a worship song thrives through the course of three centuries, we would be wise to pay attention and learn from it.

Proverbs 9:9-10 (NIV)

9 Instruct the wise and they will be wiser still;

   teach the righteous and they will add to their learning.

10 The fear of the Lord is the beginning of wisdom,

and knowledge of the Holy One is understanding.

Song Idea

What are some non-biblical words or non-religious words you could use to convey a biblical act of extravagant worship? Write your ideas below. You may want to visit a thesaurus.

Song Hook

Craft your best idea above into an invitational song hook.

Songwriting Tip

Pay attention to your conversational tone. Is it formal or casual? Is it classic or modern? Strong songwriters make it their goal to keep a consistent conversational tone throughout the entire lyric.

Title:

Music and Lyrics by:

Title:

Music and Lyrics by:

Week 34
Write an Adoration Song

Inspiration

In the Book of Esther, we read the account of a high king calling for his queen to stand before the people. The queen refused and was ultimately replaced by Queen Esther. One of the concepts we see in Esther is that intimacy must be balanced with majesty. Queen Esther understood that her lover was also her king. I think sometimes it's important to remember this in modern worship circles as well. At times, our intimacy with God — that is, the sense of His nearness, His favor, and his love — can tempt us to get too casual in our approach to Him. Christ's blood has given us confident access, and we are His beloved bride; however, we are still approaching the King of the universe. Take time to meditate on His majesty and how God is reverenced by the heavenly hosts.

Psalm 89:6-7 (NIV)

6 For who in the skies above can compare with the Lord?

Who is like the Lord among the heavenly beings?

7 In the council of the holy ones God is greatly feared;

he is more awesome than all who surround him.

Song Idea

Compose a list of words and images that describes the majesty and awesomeness of God in the space below.

Song Hook

Your assignment this week is to compose a song that captures the concept of His majesty. Craft an adoration song hook that inspires this sense of awe and reverent worship.

Songwriting Tip

If your songs all start sounding the same, try changing song forms (e.g. from Verse/Chorus to AAA), time signature (e.g. from 4/4 to 6/8), or use different musical genres and instruments to inspire fresh approaches to your songwriting.

Title:

Music and Lyrics by:

Title:

Music and Lyrics by:

Week 35
Write a Petition Song

Inspiration

Jesus prayed, "Lead us not into temptation and deliver us from evil." No one will live without trials and temptations, but, evidently, prayers can keep some of these hardships from coming your way. Many of us only pray retroactively rather than proactively. We pray after the waters of trial have already risen to flood stage. I'm sure most people cried out to God from the rising waters of Noah's flood, but only those who had sought the Lord beforehand found themselves safe and protected in the ark.

Psalm 32:6-7 (NIV)

6 Therefore let all the faithful pray to you while you may be found; surely the rising of the mighty waters will not reach them. 7 You are my hiding place; you will protect me from

trouble and surround me with songs of deliverance.

Song Idea

Create a list of some of the things God has already delivered you out of. Make another list of things you are seeking the Lord for deliverance from.

Song Hook

Craft a song hook that is a prayer for deliverance.

Songwriting Tip

Make sure the rhythm and melody on your verses and chorus are not too similar. Contrasting in melody, rhythm, and lyric while maintaining a single theme is a key to great songwriting.

Title:

Music and Lyrics by:

Title:

Music and Lyrics by:

Week 36
Write a Declaration Song

Inspiration

Physics, history, and Scripture agree that words have incredible destructive and healing properties. Jesus used words on several occasions to heal and deliver sick bodies (Psalm 107:20, Matthew 8:8, 8:16, and Luke 7:7). I have personally seen two women who were crippled for years rise and walk after breaking off word curses and receiving the healing words of Jesus. If we truly knew the power of our words, we would treat them more like a loaded weapon. There is much in the world we could complain about or protest, but our words are meant to bring life and healing.

Proverbs 12:18 (NIV)

The words of the reckless pierce like swords, but the tongue of the wise brings healing.

Song Idea

Write a list of words or phrases that bring healing to minds, bodies, or relationships. Your list can contain simple ideas like "I'm sorry," "You're forgiven," or "It wasn't your fault."

Song Hook

Craft a song hook that releases a healing declaration in the space below.

Songwriting Tip

Melodic emphasis is discovered by analyzing which word of your chorus or song hook has the highest or longest note. This emphasis in the melody line can drastically change the meaning of your song. Try altering your melodic emphasis several times by singing each word of your song hook as the highest note until you have found the strongest melody to enforce the message of your song.

Title:

Music and Lyrics by:

Title:

Music and Lyrics by:

Week 37
Write an Invitation Song

Inspiration

Invitations carry with them an amazing power of affirmation. Whenever you are invited somewhere—even if you don't end up going—you feel included and honored at having been asked. Perhaps this is why the invitation to "come" is used over 1,200 times in Scripture. God wants to affirm your place in His family and kingdom. He wants you to know that you belong and are desired. Where is God currently inviting you to come?

Isaiah 55:1 (NIV)

Come, all you who are thirsty, come to the waters;

and you who have no money, come, buy and eat!

Come, buy wine and milk without money and without cost.

Song Idea

Worship songs often use word pictures to communicate truth. This week as you focus on invitations to come, you can convey them with word pictures like "Come to the rock," "Come to the waters," or "Come to the table." Create a list of word pictures for places God might invite us to.

Song Hook

Take your favorite idea from the list above and craft a song hook of invitation in the space below.

Songwriting Tip

The purpose of a verse is to convey context, content, and vital information. The purpose of a chorus is to feature the song hook. Great songwriters craft verses that convey only the most vital information for setting the stage for your feature idea — the song hook.

Title:

Music and Lyrics by:

157

Title:

Music and Lyrics by:

Week 38
Write an Adoration Song

Inspiration

Two weeks ago, we examined the power of our words to heal or destroy. This week, we will focus on the revelation of Christ himself as Healer. When God heals someone, He is not just doing something, He is *being* who He is.

Exodus 15:26b and Psalm 103:2-3 (NIV)

26b "...I am the Lord, who heals you."

2 Praise the Lord, my soul,

   and forget not all his benefits—
3 who forgives all your sins

   and heals all your diseases

Song Idea

Your assignment this week is not to ask God for healing (petition), nor declare what He can do (declaration), neither is it to invite people to be healed (invitation). This week we will simply honor and worship Him as Healer (adoration). What are some of the areas of healing you want to target?

Song Hook

Compose an adoration song about Christ the Healer without using the words "heal," "healing," or "healer." Craft your main idea into a song hook in the space below.

Songwriting Tip

Melodic range refers to the distance between notes. When composing a memorable melody, great songwriters consider the strength or limitations of their audience's vocal range.

Title:

Music and Lyrics by:

Title:

Music and Lyrics by:

Week 39
Write a Petition Song

Inspiration

I love verses 29-31 in Acts 4. The believers had already been filled with the Spirit on the Day of Pentecost. They were preaching with boldness and doing miracles. However, here in chapter four, they pray for more of what they already have, and God shakes the place with His power. What I currently have does not limit what I can have in God. His greatness is unsearchable; what God is offering is infinitely beyond my human capacity to fully contain. With this understanding, I can always grow and increase in my encounters and expressions of His goodness.

Acts 4:29-31(NIV)

29 Now, Lord, consider their threats and enable your servants to speak your word with great boldness. **30** Stretch out your hand to heal and perform signs and wonders through the name of your holy servant Jesus." **31** After they prayed, the place where they were meeting was shaken. And they were all filled with the Holy Spirit and spoke the word of God boldly.

Song Idea

What did it feel like when you were baptized with the Holy Spirit? (If you haven't had this experience, I encourage you to ask Him for it.) What things have you seen God do through you since He filled you? In what areas are you crying out for a fresh infilling of the Holy Spirit?

Song Hook

Craft a song hook around a petition for a fresh filling of the Holy Spirit and power.

Songwriting Tip

Great writers do not include song parts or lyrics that don't contribute to the overall forward motion of their song. Sometimes we fall in love with a great line, catchy melody, or intriguing song section that truly doesn't fit the flow of the song we are crafting. Disappointing as it can be, it is best to extract these sections and feature them in another song more consistent with their value.

Title:

Music and Lyrics by:

Title:

Music and Lyrics by:

Week 40
Write a Declaration Song

Inspiration

Remembering or reflecting on what God has done for you in the past gives you courage to face your present and future difficulties. Such meditations also keep us in a place of thanksgiving and rejoicing. Our testimony is part of our confidence (1 Samuel 17:34), our armor (Ephesians 6:15), and our prophetic ability to recreate similar breakthroughs (Revelation 19:10).

Isaiah 63:7 (NIV)

I will tell of the kindnesses of the Lord, the deeds for which he is to be praised, according to all the Lord has done for us—yes, the many good things he has done for Israel, according to his compassion and many kindnesses.

Song Idea

Make bullet points of some of the things you have heard, seen, and experienced of God's goodness towards you and those around you.

Song Hook

Let your above ideas inspire verse material for your strong testimony song hook.

Songwriting Tip

Melodic motif refers to a catchy bit of melody, harmony, or rhythm in your song. This phrase may be different from your main song hook and appear several times throughout the song in various forms. Proper use of a melodic motif helps make your song memorable.

Title:

Music and Lyrics by:

Title:

Music and Lyrics by:

Week 41
Write an Invitation Song

Inspiration

The following verse talks about spurring one another on toward love and good deeds. A spur is a small spiked wheel that is worn on a rider's heel used for urging a horse forward. In Greek, the word can mean "to provoke, to irritate, or to make sharp." God encourages us to provoke one another to keep pressing toward the target of love and good deeds. A song can be a great spur — a reminder to press on in this way — because the melody and accompanying words can stick in our thoughts all day long.

Hebrews 10:23-24 (NIV)

23 Let us hold unswervingly to the hope we profess, for he who promised is faithful. 24 And let us consider how we may spur one another on toward love and good deeds,

Song Idea

This week's assignment is to create an invitation song that spurs you and others towards love and good deeds. Choose the specific target of love you will be aiming towards and write it below.

Song Hook

By now, you are getting good at crafting your larger ideas into a clear and concise song hook. Write this invitation song hook below.

Songwriting Tip

What do you do if your song sounds like someone else's song? First, ask the question, "How much of it is similar?" Usually, you will want your song to be at least 60% unique. If your song is too similar, consider changing tempo, time signature, or song form to reinvent a more original sound.

Title:

Music and Lyrics by:

Title:

Music and Lyrics by:

Week 42
Write an Adoration Song

Inspiration

Jesus had an amazing ability to hang out with "sinners" without engaging in their stuff. He seemed to prefer the outcasts above the religious order of His day. I think about how different we are in this way; the church of our day has not often been accused of being "the friend of sinners." Perhaps an adoration song focused on Jesus' compassion for the lost and broken will restore our own hearts and vision for those Christ died for.

Matthew 11:19 (NIV)

19 The Son of Man came eating and drinking, and they say, "Here is a glutton and a drunkard, a friend of tax collectors and sinners." But wisdom is proved right by her deeds.

Song Idea

What are some of the personal qualities that made Jesus appealing to the non-religious crowd? List them in the space below.

Song Hook

Craft an adoration song hook based on one of the qualities you listed above.

Songwriting Tip

The title of your song is important. People will search for your song by the perceived title, which is often the same as your song hook. If you get overly clever with your title and make it drastically different than your song hook, it may be hard for people to find your song when searching for it.

Title:

Music and Lyrics by:

Title:

Music and Lyrics by:

Week 43
Freestyle Writing

Inspiration

Congratulations! You have hit another mile marker in your songwriting journey. As you enter the last quarter of your one-year commitment, you only have ten songs left to compose, including this one. With each song you write, you are greatly expanding your personal worship vocabulary. Your retention of biblical concepts, Scripture, and the attributes of God is definitely increasing. By now, your prayer life and call to worship are merging together in a shared force. And in the midst of all your spiritual growth, you are really honing your song craft. Now it is time to use what you have learned to finish strong. It's not how you start the race that determines your rewards but how you finish.

Acts 20:24 (NIV)

"...my only aim is to finish the race and complete the task the Lord Jesus has given me—the task of testifying to the good news of God's grace."

Song Idea

Which type of worship song has been easiest for you to compose? Why do you think that is? Consider this week taking on the worship song type that is hardest for you to write just for the purpose of strengthening your skills. Write in the space below what God is currently speaking to you about. How would you craft these ideas into the song type that has been most difficult for you?

Song Hook

Craft a song hook from your best song idea.

Songwriting Tip

Great songwriters expect to rewrite their songs several times. Don't confuse a finished draft with a finished song. Be open to revisions and input that will make your song stronger.

Title:

Music and Lyrics by:

Title:

Music and Lyrics by:

Week 44
Write a Petition Song

Inspiration

It's important that our prayers not only focus on our own wants or needs. Intercession for others keeps our hearts from getting self-centered and careless. The same should be true in our song craft. Rather than just writing from your own voice, learn how to give a voice in songwriting to people with different needs, visions, and points-of-view.

Psalm 122:6 (NIV)

6 Pray for the peace of Jerusalem:

"May those who love you be secure.

Song Idea

What city do you have a burden for? What things do you want to see happen in that city? What is your prayer for the people of that city? Write your thoughts below.

Song Hook

Craft a petition song hook around intercession for a city.

Songwriting Tip

Co-writing is also a key to improving your songwriting. There is strength in numbers and wisdom in the counsel of many. Sometimes the best way to rise to the next level of songwriting is to partner with the strengths of someone else and get a fresh critique on your own ideas.

Title:

Music and Lyrics by:

Title:

Music and Lyrics by:

Week 45
Write a Declaration Song

Inspiration

One of the great truths of the Bible is that God removed our stuff so we could have His stuff. He exchanged His righteousness for our sin. Righteousness is no longer something to try to become. Through Christ, it is now something you are. Acts of righteousness come from your new identity, from your personal identification with Jesus Christ. Your assignment this week will be to craft a corporate identity declaration based on this biblical truth.

2 Corinthians 5:21 (NIV)

God made him who had no sin to be sin for us, so that in him we might become the righteousness of God.

Song Idea

We are the righteousness of God in Jesus Christ. Righteousness is not necessarily an easy word to sing or understand. How might you craft this amazing concept into something more singable? Write your ideas below.

Song Hook

A corporate identity song hook will often start with words like, "We are...." Write your song hook idea in the space below.

Songwriting Tip

Once you understand song craft, you can analyze your favorite songs to find out what makes them great. Use the knowledge of strong songwriting you have gained to determine the building blocks your favorite writers use that most communicate to you. With this understanding, you can write songs that you like.

Title:

Music and Lyrics by:

Title:

Music and Lyrics by:

Week 46
Write an Invitation Song

Inspiration

Humility is one of the defining character traits of Jesus Christ and His followers. The author C.S. Lewis said that the problem with pride is that it keeps you looking down on people and things. When you are looking down, you cannot see what is above you. Making less of yourself than what is true is false humility; making more of yourself than you ought to is pride. Perhaps humility is really found in knowing who you would be apart from the grace and righteousness of Christ.

James 4:10 (NIV)

Humble yourselves before the Lord, and he will lift you up.

Song Idea

How can we call each other to the true humility that attracts the favor of God? Write your thoughts below.

Song Hook

Craft a song hook around the call to humility.

Songwriting Tip

Most people find it difficult to refine while they create. Both refining and creating are necessary components to the larger creative process, yet great writers learn to capture creative ideas while they are freely flowing and save refining and rewriting for a later time.

Title:

Music and Lyrics by:

Copyright is Today's Date:

Title:

Music and Lyrics by:

Week 47
Write an Adoration Song

Inspiration

Isaiah and John the Revelator both had the same picture of the throne room of heaven. Around the throne, the four seraphim are uniquely equipped to worship God. Covered with eyes, they have unlimited perspective of the One who sits on the throne. With different faces, they can view the Lord through different lenses. They can fly and hover to view the Lord from unique angles. Yet with all of this special worship equipment, their primary focus is on how holy He is. When was the last time you allowed yourself to be vulnerable to the weight of the holiness of God?

Isaiah 6:1-3 (NIV)

1 "...I saw the Lord, high and exalted, seated on a throne; and the train of his robe filled the temple. 2 Above him were seraphim, each with six wings: With two wings they covered

their faces, with two they covered their feet, and with two they were flying. **3** And they were calling to one another: "Holy, holy, holy is the Lord Almighty; the whole earth is full of his glory."

Song Idea

What qualities of God inspire you to cry out, "Holy, holy"? In the space below, create word pictures that inspire that sense of awe and wonder.

Song Hook

Craft an adoration song hook focused on the holiness of God.

Songwriting Tip:

Songwriters Pete and Pat Lubboff recommend, "Don't force a song to fit your reality; let it have its own integrity." If you only write from what you have experienced, then you will rarely encounter something new. Write about what is true, and let your experience rise to the level of your declaration.

Title:

Music and Lyrics by:

Title:

Music and Lyrics by:

Week 48
Write a Petition Song

Inspiration

I thought it appropriate that your last prayer song of the year should be inspired by the first prayer Jesus taught.

Matthew 6:9-13 (NIV)

9 "This, then, is how you should pray: 'Our Father in heaven, hallowed be your name, 10 your kingdom come, your will be done, on earth as it is in heaven. 11 Give us today our daily bread. 12 And forgive us our debts, as we also have forgiven our debtors. 13 And lead us not into temptation, but deliver us from the evil one.

Song Idea

There are three basic types of Scripture songs: 1) literal —
where you sing the words exactly how they appear, 2)
adapted — where you paraphrase the Scripture to fit your
conversational tone and lyrical meter, and 3) inspired —
where you take the concept of a specific passage but add
supporting ideas and lyrics to the biblical text. Choose one of
these three Scripture song forms to craft your version of The
Lord's Prayer.

Song Hook

Even a literal Scripture song has a song hook. What line or
phrase of these verses are the focal point of your song? Craft
that into your hook.

Songwriting Tip

Song craft and structure is a faithful servant but can also be a
cruel master. Now that you have learned and mastered some
tools of song craft, let them serve you rather than limit your
creativity.

Title:

Music and Lyrics by:

Title:

Music and Lyrics by:

Week 49
Write a Declaration Song

Inspiration

Jesus commanded His disciples to preach that the kingdom of Heaven is here (Matthew 10:7-8). I can think of no greater message for your last declaration song of the year than the primary message of Jesus and His disciples. The New Testament is filled with the qualities and characteristics of His kingdom.

Romans 14:7 (NIV)

"For the kingdom of God is not a matter of eating and drinking, but of righteousness, peace and joy in the Holy Spirit,"

Song Idea

What are some primary things about the kingdom of Heaven that you like to focus on? Write your answers below.

Song Hook

Craft your ideas into a single declaration of the nearness and availability of the kingdom of Heaven.

Songwriting Tip

Worship writers should always check the doctrine of their lyrics with pastors, teachers, and leaders. We want to partner with leadership for a healthy doxology in the church.

Title:

Music and Lyrics by:

Title:

Music and Lyrics by:

Week 50
Write an Invitation Song

Inspiration

In the late 1800's, young Judson Van De Venter had mastered 13 different instruments. He sang and composed songs and was very involved in the music ministry at his Methodist Episcopal church. He was also a gifted teacher. Eventually, he found himself torn between his successful teaching career and his desire to be a part of an evangelistic team. The struggle lasted five years. In 1896, while conducting the music for a worship service, Van De Venter surrendered his desires completely to God and became a vocational evangelist. Out of that struggle, a song was born in his heart that has been sung in churches now for more than 120 years: the classic hymn "I Surrender All." Following Jesus requires a total surrender to His goodness.

Matthew 4:19-22 (NIV)

19 "Come, follow me," Jesus said, "and I will send you out to fish for people." **20** At once they left their nets and followed him. **21** Going on from there, he saw two other brothers, James son of Zebedee and his brother John. They were in a boat with their father Zebedee, preparing their nets. Jesus called them, **22** and immediately they left the boat and their father and followed him.

Song Idea

Van De Venter was a church musician and songwriter, yet he still struggled to surrender all to God. Are there any areas you wrestle with in surrendering fully to God? Write down what they are.

Song Hook

Craft a song hook that is an invitation or call to total surrender.

Songwriting Tip

A worship song is finished when other people are consistently carried into His presence while singing it. Until then, consider that it could be made stronger.

Title:

Music and Lyrics by:

_____

_____

_____

_____

_____

_____

_____

_____

_____

_____

_____

_____

_____

_____

_____

_____

_____

Copyright is Today's Date:

Title:

Music and Lyrics by:

Week 51
Write an Adoration Song

Inspiration

This is your final adoration song of the year. Just think of how focusing on the character and nature of God through adoration songs has caused you to know Him better and experience more of His goodness. You have shown yourself faithful to complete this year of writing a worship song every week. Now, let's celebrate His faithfulness to you.

1 Corinthians 1:8-9 (NIV)

8 "He will also keep you firm to the end, so that you will be blameless on the day of our Lord Jesus Christ. 9 God is faithful, who has called you into fellowship with his Son, Jesus Christ our Lord."

Song Idea

There are so many ways that God demonstrates His faithfulness in our lives. Write down a few of the areas where He has been faithful to you.

Song Hook

Craft your adoration song hook around this theme of God as faithful.

Songwriting Tip

When testing a worship song for the first time with a small group or congregation, listen carefully to how they sing it. If there are places where they drop out or change the melody, then consider rewriting the song accordingly. The congregation's version is probably the more singable approach to a strong congregational worship song.

Title:

Music and Lyrics by:

Title:

Music and Lyrics by:

Week 52
Rewriting Exercise

Inspiration

Congratulations! You are about to complete the one-year worship writing journal. You've discovered the concept through this journal that great songs are not just written; they are rewritten. The Lord spoke to the prophet Habakkuk that he was to write down his revelations and make them plain so that other people could run with them. The refining and rewriting process is how we make our revelations plain so that other people can benefit from the songs we write. It is our commitment to hear from the Lord and the people. The worship writer is a servant to both God and man. That is why we are willing to rewrite and refine our revelations — so they can serve the people in the worship of God.

Habakkuk 2:2 (NIV)

Then the Lord replied: "Write down the revelation and make it plain on tablets so that a runner may run with it.

Song Idea

For our final worship writing assignment, leaf back through the pages of your journal and look for what you consider to be your weakest song. Using what you have learned over the last 12 months, analyze why this song is weak. What would make it better?

Song Hook

Would you use the same song hook or re-craft it? Write your former or improved song hook here.

Songwriting Tip

People ask me a lot of questions about copyrighting their songs. This paragraph is extracted directly from the Library of Congress government copyright website:

> Under the present copyright law, which became effective January 1, 1978, a work is automatically protected by copyright when it is created. A work is created when it is "fixed" or embodied in a copy or phonorecord for the first time. Neither registration in the Copyright Office nor publication is required for copyright protection under the law.

Title:

Music and Lyrics by:

Title:

Music and Lyrics by:

Congratulations!
You have completed the fifty-two week worship writing journal!

Stop and take time to meditate on your accomplishment. You can truly call yourself a worship writer now. You have composed over fifty songs based on Scriptural ideas and inspirations. What do you consider to be your top five songs of the year?

1.

2.

3.

4.

5.

I recommend revisiting these five songs to see if there is anything you have learned throughout the year that could make them even stronger. Rewriting your best songs into even greater songs can be a really wise discipline. Consider finding a regular co-writing partner to help you with critique and rewrites. A fresh set of eyes and ears can do wonders for the strength of a song.

On the following page, I have shared some bonus material regarding what you can do now with your best compositions. Before you move on, I would like to recommend that you consider continuing your habit of writing a song each week. You can repeat the assignments in this journal, create your own year of songwriting assignments, or try one of my other songwriting journals available from Amazon.com or MissionVacaville.org.

Congratulations again on your amazing accomplishment, and may God continue to grace you to serve your local community and the world beyond with great worship writing.

Dano

Dan McCollam

Bonus Material
What to do with a "finished"
song

1. Make sure it consistently takes you somewhere in
    your private worship times.

2. Bring it to pastors, teachers, or church leaders who
    can review the lyrical content for doctrinal accuracy
    to help determine the season of the song. Be open to
    rewrites from their suggestions. Your openness and
    teachability is really important to strengthening this
    relationship and getting truly helpful feedback in the
    future.

3. Share it in a small group setting such as a Bible study,
    home group, or prayer meeting to see if the song has

a positive effect on the group. Listen for possible re-writes of the lyric and melody based upon how quickly the group can catch on and sing it. Invite feedback from the group members for possible improvements to your song.

4. Share your song with a member or members of your church worship team. I suggest that a new song be introduced first as a pre-service warm up, offering number, or during an altar time. This gets your congregation familiar with the song without necessarily having to sing along in focused worship. Then, if it gets positive feedback, enter it into the worship set. If people haven't caught on to the song after the third time you introduce it in a worship set, then consider that it is either the wrong season, the wrong setting, or the song needs more work.

5. If there is a positive response in your own church, then it might be time to copyright the song. You can copyright it yourself by recording it to a fixed media data. Though it is not necessary, you might feel more secure by filing with the Library of Congress copyright office or use one of the many online services to do the copyright for you. At this point, you have determined that the song is in its final form and you are ready to share the song with other churches you are in fellowship with. Consider making a rough demo and chord chart so the song can be distributed to others. You might also want to register the song now with Christian Copyright Licensing International (CCLI).

6. Make a YouTube lyric or performance video of the song and post a link on websites and social media.

7. Consider entering your song in a contest. Song contests are typically easy to find with an internet web search.

8. If an artist asks to record your song, I recommend that you let him or her. The more publicity the song gets the better.

9. When using a studio or producer for the first time to record a song, it is best to contract for a single song. That way you can evaluate your creative chemistry before committing to the time and expense of a full project.

10. If someone offers you an artist agreement or contract for your songs, spend the time and money to have a lawyer look at the contract to make sure it is a favorable agreement.

The Worship Writer's Guide
By Dan McCollam

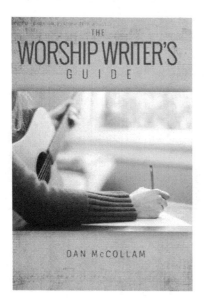

The Worship Writer's Guide gives you fourteen transformational tools for writing great praise and worship songs. The powerful lyrical and melodic techniques contained in this book will help you tap into the wisdom that will strengthen the quality of your songwriting regardless of the style or genre.

Finding Your Song
By Dan McCollam

Finding Your Song explores seven sources of inspiration for writing great praise and worship songs. Whether you are a first-timer or trying to bust through a creative block, the practical exercises and creative starters in this book will enlarge your journey as a worship writer.

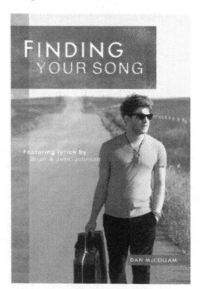

A Song for Seven Mountains
A 52-Week Songwriting Journal for Marketplace Writers

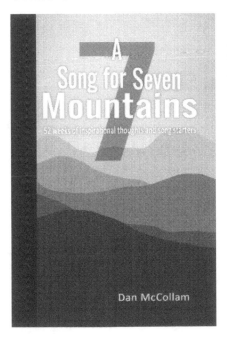

Discover your primary musical sphere of influence as you practice writing songs for government, education, media, arts & entertainment, business, family, and religion. Be inspired in your art through Scripture and songwriting tips as well as the success stories of award-winning writers.

By Dan McCollam

Worship Writer's Songwriting Course
a 12-lesson course in MP3 format
By Dan McCollam

Worship Writers Songwriting Course is a 12-part MP3 audio teaching in a live radio show format that equips you to write great praise and worship songs.

Also included are all of the teaching notes and 30 songwriting assignments in PDF format for an interactive songwriting experience.

You can find resources
by Dan McCollam at
http://store.imissionchurch.com/

or

https://shop.ibethel.org/

or

Amazon.com

<u>Other books by Dan McCollam</u>

Basic Training for Prophetic Activation

Prophetic Company

My Super Powers
a children's series on gifts of the Holy Spirit

Made in the USA
Lexington, KY
30 August 2018